grace MINUTE

Finding Your *Rest*
in the Love of Jesus

GREGORY T. RIETHER

Greg Riether Ministries
8177 S. Harvard Ave #330
Tulsa, Oklahoma
Printed in the United States of America

First Edition: January 2018
10 9 8 7 6 5 4 3 2 1

ISBN: 978-1-937250-78-2

This Book is Presented to:

_____

on:

_____

Contents

Foreword

Every believer in Jesus Christ is in the process of learning and believing the truth about who God is, what He is like, and what He has done for us in Jesus. John 1:18 reads, "*No one has seen God at any time. The only begotten Son, who is in the bosom of the Father, He has declared Him.*" This means that before Jesus arrived, we did not have an accurate view of what God was really like or how He really felt toward us. It took Jesus, who came right from the heart of God (His bosom), to reveal the character and intentions of God. And what Jesus revealed is astounding! So much so, that it requires us to change our default ways of thinking about God and how we relate to Him.

God doesn't think like we think! His thoughts are so much higher, so much better, so much more loving and good than we could have ever imag-

ined! Jesus came to reveal this and to permanently remove the barrier of sin that kept us from being able to partake of the Father's goodness, love, and blessing. In Jesus, you have become eternally worthy of God's blessing and favor.

As believers in Christ, our minds need washed from wrong thinking and wrong believing that hold us in the bondage of feeling unworthy and separated from God. We need to be established in the new default way of thinking of the Kingdom of God! God's way of thinking will bring you joy, love, peace, and victory!

These devotions are designed to recenter your mind on God's way of thinking. They are short but poignant truths that Jesus eternally established for you in the New Covenant. I fervently desire that they help to ground you in the mind and heart of your heavenly Father.

— Gregory Riether

God Is *Love*

"There is no fear in love; but perfect love casts out fear, because fear involves torment. But he who fears has not been made perfect in love."

—*1 John 4:18*

First John 4:8 says, "God is love." God doesn't just *possess* love. He *is* love. It is part of His being. I have a wooden dresser at home. If I were to take the wood out of the dresser, it would no longer be a dresser. If you took the love out of God, I don't know who you would be talking about, but it wouldn't be God anymore. The more you understand that He is love and that *you are* the object of His love, the more your fear in life will diminish. The Bible says that His perfect love casts out fear. This verse is really talking about the fear of God's punishment; therefore, the more that you, as a believer in Jesus, understand that God is love, the more your fear of God will diminish. But this diminishment of fear applies to all areas of your life. Are you afraid of anything today? Don't focus on getting more faith to overcome the fear; focus on His love. Galatians 5:6 says that *faith worketh by love.* The more you meditate on how much He loves you, the more your faith will be strengthened. The more you meditate on His love for you, the more your fear will diminish. If you're having to face down something tough this week, remember, you have a Father, and He loves you.

. . . .

Prayer of Agreement

Father, I will believe what You say about who You are. I will believe that You are love, and that Your love is constantly directed toward me. I receive Your love and I'm secure in Your love. As I embrace this in meditation before You, I am looking for all my fears to diminish. Thank You for loving me all the time.

You Are Wired to
Run on Approval

"He chose us in Him before the foundation of the world, that we should be holy and without blame before Him in love."

—*Ephesians 1:4*

Do you sometimes wish that you weren't such a people pleaser? Maybe you think, *I'm always the one who is bending over backward for others, but others don't seem to do the same for me.* There's a resentment toward people that can build inside of you when you live this way. What may be behind this desire to please others in such a one-sided way is a need to get others to approve of you. You're really looking to feel good about yourself by seeking the approval of others. Do you know that humans are hard-wired by God to run on approval? It's just that God wired us to find our completeness in *His* approval, not in the approval of others. We are complete when we know that God approves of us. And here's the wonderful news of the Gospel: *You are complete in Jesus!* God approves of you! Ephesians 1:6 says that you are accepted in the Beloved. In Jesus, you are always approved. Always. You can stop seeking approval; you have it. Live your life in the joy of this approval.

. . . .

Prayer of Agreement

Father, I believe what You say about me, that I am accepted and approved of by You. Thank You that You made me complete in Jesus and, just like Jesus, I am Your beloved child in whom You are well-pleased . . . all the time.

Jesus Wants to Immerse You in His Identity

"Go therefore and make disciples of all the nations, baptizing them in the name of the Father and of the Son and of the Holy Spirit." —*Matthew 28:19*

Jesus wants you to make a radical change in the way you think about yourself. He gave the disciples the instruction to baptize (which means "to immerse") people into a new identity. He said, "*baptize them <u>into</u>* (the Greek word here is *eis*, meaning 'into') *the name of* (the identity of) *the Father, Son, and Holy Spirit.*" The Lord's instruction is to immerse people into the identity of the Father, Son, and Spirit. Baptism is all about receiving the truth of who you are now in Jesus. Romans 6:3–4 says, *"Or do you not know that as* *many of us as were baptized into Christ Jesus were baptized into His death? Therefore we were buried with Him through baptism into death, that just as Christ was raised from the dead by the glory of the Father, even so we also should walk in newness of life."* Baptism is the sign that you are joined, as one, to Jesus. When He died, you died. When He was raised, you were raised. This leads us into a brand-new way to live. The Christian life is not about you striving to be a better person. It's about you recognizing that you are already like Him because He has made Himself one with you. *"As He is, so are we in this world!"* You have His life in you! You have been immersed into the family name.

. . . .

Prayer of Agreement

Jesus, I believe what You say about me, that I have been joined as one with You. Thank You for the unspeakable privilege of being part of Your family! Holy Spirit, please remind me today of who I really am: a son/daughter of my loving, good Father.

God Is Not Mad
at You

"For this is like the waters of Noah to Me; for as I have sworn that the waters of Noah would no longer cover the earth, so have I sworn that I would not be angry with you, nor rebuke you." —*Isaiah 54:9*

I once was speaking before a group of men, and I asked them, "How many of you believe that God may be angry with you today?" Nearly every man in the room raised his hand. These were believers in Jesus! I felt a great compassion in my heart because, twelve years ago, I would have raised my hand with them. What a place of despair that is! I was able to tell these precious brothers the incredible truth of the New Covenant in Jesus, that God says clearly, *"I will never be angry with you or rebuke you."* Never! You may be wondering today if God is angry with you for something you've done, or maybe you fear you might be under

His wrath. Listen to the truth: He has promised in His Word to *"never be angry with you or rebuke you."* He is not dealing with you according to your iniquities, nor is He even remembering your sins (see Hebrews 10:17). That's the New Covenant. The sin issue between you and God is finished. Jesus said, *"It is finished!"* Believe in the *finished work* of Jesus for you! Believe He's the Lamb of God who took away the sins of the entire world—even your sins! If your sins are gone, and He's not dealing with you according to your iniquities, then what would He be angry about? The Father is on your side. Rest in His love and favor today.

. . . .

Prayer of Agreement

Jesus, I believe what You say, that You are the Lamb of God who has taken away my sins. I believe what You say in Your Word, that You have never been angry with me, nor will You ever rebuke me. Holy Spirit, thank You for living inside of me. And thank You that You are leading me to embrace my true identity as Your righteous, worthy, holy child.

God Has Made You
One with Him

"To them God willed to make known what are the riches of the glory of this mystery among the Gentiles: which is "Christ in you, the hope of glory."
—Colossians 1:27

If you are like most people, there are some days when you feel like God is far away from you, days when your prayers don't seem to make it past the ceiling, days when you may even say out loud, "Where are You, God?" We have this picture in our minds of God sitting on His throne in heaven, and all would be well if we could just get Him to look our way. Of course, that way of thinking is all wrong. When you became a believer in Jesus, God removed all distance from you. There is no space between your spirit and His Spirit. The Bible says that we are one spirit with Him. Do you see the power of this? You are not "close" to God. "Closeness" still implies some distance and opens the possibility to be farther from Him. You are not close to God. You are one with Him (1 Corinthians 6:17). God has made for Himself a holy temple in which to dwell—and you are that temple! (1 Corinthians 3:16). God is inside of you right now. He is Emmanuel, which is to say, "God will never depart." He is in you when you do good. He is in you when you do bad. He has taken up permanent residence. Stop praying to the ceiling. Look inward. Father is in you. Jesus Himself is in you.

. . . .

Prayer of Agreement

Jesus, I will believe what You say, that You are in me forever, never to leave. The feelings I sometimes have of You being far away from me are always a lie. Thank You that You always hear my prayers. Always!

God Provides for
Your Physical Needs

"Do not trouble me; the door is now shut, and my children are with me in bed; I cannot rise and give to you."

—*Luke 11:7*

It's possible that there is a real need in your life this week. Maybe it's a need for a better job, or for a place to live, or for a car that doesn't break down. Does God care about these things? Oftentimes our spiritual solution is to bang on the doors of heaven, hoping to rouse God into action. Jesus said it perfectly in a parable: It's like God is our neighbor and we're getting Him up in the middle of the night, feeling like we're inconveniencing Him, banging on His door; hoping to get some bread. You know, that was a picture of people living under the Old Covenant. They always felt condemned and unworthy because of their inability to keep the Law of God. In that system, it felt like God was a reluctant, unfeeling neighbor on the other side of a locked door. The reality *in Jesus* is that God is our Father. He's not our neighbor. See, the father in the parable says that he is in bed with his children. Don't think that odd. In the culture of that day, with only one room in the house, the entire family slept together. Jesus was saying that this is the picture of you and your Father right now: You're not banging on the closed doors of heaven; you are curled up in bed with your heavenly Father. From that place, ask and it will be given.

. . . .

Prayer of Agreement
Father, I believe what You say about me,
that I am part of Your family. I am not the
estranged neighbor, pounding on Your door
from the outside. I am curled up, as a child, in
Your loving arms, and even my whisper cap-
tures Your attention. Thank You for giving
me everything I need. I love You, Papa.

God Is Only
Good

"If you then, being evil, know how to give good gifts to your children, how much more will your Father who is in heaven give good things to those who ask Him!"

—*Matthew 7:11*

God is so good, isn't He? He sends nothing bad your way. If it's bad, like sickness or tragedy or any of the things that come from the curse of sin in this world (see Deuteronomy 27 and 28), that's not from God. Jesus delivered us from the curse! (Galatians 3:13). The Bible says in James 1 that only good and perfect gifts come down from the Father of lights. He is good, and only good. One day, a rich, young ruler called Jesus, "Good Teacher." Jesus latched on to that word and said, *"God alone is good."* Jesus was saying that in all the universe, there is only one Being that defines what it means to be good. So much so that when you hear the word "good," as in *"good teacher,"* if you under-stand goodness like Jesus understood goodness, your mind will immediately turn full-tilt toward God. Goodness equals God. God equals goodness. If God is love and God is good, think of how safe You are with Him. God will never harm You. On the contrary, He knows how to give good gifts to His kids! Expect His goodness to show up today.

. . . .

Prayer of Agreement

Father, I believe what Jesus said when He called You "good." I believe that You only give good gifts to me. I reject all thoughts that tell me that any sickness or tragedy could ever be from You. You are my Father. Jesus, You are my deliverer! I am keeping my eyes and my heart open to Your goodness today!

God Sees You According to the *Spirit*

"Therefore, from now on, we regard no one according to the flesh. Even though we have known Christ according to the flesh, yet now we know Him thus no longer. Therefore, if anyone is in Christ, he is a new creation."

—*2 Corinthians 5:16–17*

What does God think when He looks at you? Do you think He's frustrated, disappointed, or upset at your lack of spiritual progress? A lot of believers think that way. The problem is, in viewing ourselves that way, we are regarding ourselves according to the flesh, not according to the spirit. We are judging ourselves based on fleshly deeds, not based on spirit reality. The Bible says to no longer regard *anyone* according the flesh, but to see all people according to the spirit: the truth of who people are in the spirit, in Jesus. Stop seeing yourself according to the flesh. Stop labeling yourself as just an "old sinner, saved by grace." No, that is seeing your salvation from a fleshly perspective. The spirit truth is far greater. You are a new creation in Christ. You are a son/daughter of your Father. You are the righteousness of God in Christ. You are as righteous as God is! He gave that righteousness to you as a gift. You are righteous, worthy, holy, and without blemish. That's the real you, all the time. That's how God sees you. And it's a spirit fact. Live in that!

. . . .

Prayer of Agreement

Father, I believe what You say about me, that I am a new creation in You. Help me to stop judging myself according to what I do. I choose to regard myself according to my spirit identity in Jesus. Thank You that my identity as Your new creation never changes!

23

Abide in Jesus'
Love for You

"As the Father loved Me, I also have loved you; abide in My love."

—John 15:9

It is common for believers to have this desire within them to prove out their spirituality before God. And so we do some unusual, even radical things to show God that we are serious about Him and His kingdom. We commit to getting up very early in the morning to pray, or we enter into fasts before the Lord, or we commit to reading ten chapters a day from the Bible, or we go to church services many times in a week. There's nothing wrong with doing any of those things. But the height of spirituality can never be found in something you do. Rather, it's only found in receiving what God has done for you. To those who wanted to do the work of God, Jesus answered, *"This is the work of God, that you believe in Him whom He sent"* (John 6:29). Our work is to believe Jesus. Will you believe Him? Here is Jesus' command to you: "Abide in My love." Abiding in His love is realizing that He loves you first, apart from anything you do for Him. It is becoming consciously aware that you are truly loved all of the time apart from your behavior. Do you desire to be spiritual? Wonderful! The most spiritual thing you can do today is to let God love you. And here is *great* faith: believing that God loves and favors you, even when you've done something wrong.

. . . .

Prayer of Agreement

Father, I believe what You say about me, that You love me. Today, I let go of my striving to prove my spirituality to You. I choose instead to abide in Your love for me, and then to let Your Spirit lead me to live out of Your love. You are so wonderful, Father!

25

God Is at Peace
toward Your Life

"Peace I leave with you, My peace I give to you; not as the world gives do I give to you. Let not your heart be troubled, neither let it be afraid."

—*John 14:27*

There are so many things going on in life. It can be a stressful thing to try to get everything done and squeeze everything in. We can have the mindset that "as soon as I am caught up . . . as soon as I meet my deadlines . . . as soon as these issues are resolved . . . *then* my life will be at peace." Hey, wait a minute, has that *ever* happened? Call me if it does, beacuse I want to get on that island with you! In reality, most of us are looking for a peace that the world gives, hoping that, when it comes, we'll finally be at rest. But Jesus says, "*My peace I*

give, not as the world gives it." His peace is different. His peace is something you receive by faith.
Here is how it works: He is at peace *toward* you.
He is at peace over your life. He has reconciled
you to Himself. He has overcome the world for
you, and He has solutions and paths available
through every difficulty. He's not wringing His
hands in worry over the issues of your life. See
Him at peace toward you. He bids you to behold
Him at peace over your life, and to enter His
peace.

. . . .

Prayer of Agreement

*Jesus, I believe what You say, that You are
at peace toward me and toward my life. I
choose to "let not my heart be troubled" because I choose to enter into Your peace over
me. Thank You that, no matter what is going
on in my life, I can walk in peace.*

You Have Never
Disappointed God

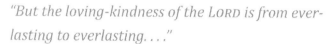

"But the loving-kindness of the LORD is from ever-lasting to everlasting. . . ."

—*Psalm 103:17*

I have to tell you, I used to struggle with the sense that my life was a disappointment to God. I felt that I had made so many bad decisions, whenever God would look at me, He would just shake His head. I thought that the only reason He accepted me and loved me was because *He had to*, based on what Jesus had done for me. Do you sometimes feel that way? Please hear the truth. God has never been disappointed with you. Not one single day. Disappointment requires that God had expectations of you that you did not meet. Please understand that God, who is omniscient (all-knowing), has never had unrealistic expectations of you. The Bible says He knew you from before the day you were born (see Psalm 139:13). He knew the measure of your days, from beginning to end. He knew every decision you would make. Every depth of sin. Every one. He saw it all, and He loved you. He *so loved* you. In fact, Psalm 103 says that His love for you had no beginning point and has no end point; it is *"from everlasting to everlasting."* He doesn't tolerate you. He loves you. He came to take away your mistakes in life, and you are eternally forgiven in Jesus, accepted and favored. You are His child, and He is pleased with you.

. . . .

Prayer of Agreement
Father, I believe what You say about me: that I am loved from everlasting to everlasting; that I am not defined as a perpetual disappointment to You; that You rejoice over my life. Today I will receive Your pleasure over me, and abide in Your great love.

You Don't Have to *Worry about Your Children*

Are you worried about your children today? Do you worry about how they are doing at school, or are you worried about their salvation, or about them making a life for themselves in the world? Do you know that your Father does not want you to be worried for them? He's a Father. He understands. That's why He told us that the covenant of His love extends to our children. Acts 2:39 says, *"The promise is to you and to your children and to all who are afar off."* Did you read that? The promise is even for our children *"who are afar off."* Isaiah 54:13 says, *"All your children shall be taught by the* L*ORD*, *and great shall be the peace of your children."* Our Father said that He will teach our children. He will bring them into His peace. Listen, your belief in this promise releases the kingdom into your children. Consider your children right now in your mind. Believe that you and the Father are together beholding them. From your parent heart, speak out and declare goodness, protection, and provision over their lives. The Father is with you in this. Release them into His care, and let go of your worry for them.

. . . .

Prayer of Agreement

Father, I believe what You say about my children, that You are establishing them before You. Even when I don't see the immediate results, I choose to believe that You are influencing them and that you will never give up on them. I continue to release them into Your loving care, and I embrace Your peace.

Have You Received
the Gift of Righteousness?

"But now the righteousness of God apart from the law is revealed, being witnessed by the Law and the Prophets, even the righteousness of God, through faith in Jesus Christ, to all and on all who believe."

—*Romans 3:21–22*

The single most important issue in your relationship with God, the one thing you must embrace before you can receive anything else from God, is the fact that Jesus has made you eternally righteous. Jesus said, *"Seek first the Kingdom of God and His righteousness and everything else will be added unto you."* Seek His righteousness, not yours. His righteousness is given as a pure gift. Romans 5:17 says that it is through the abundance of grace and the *gift* of righteousness that we reign in life. How do you reign in life? By receiving the abundance of grace and the gift of righteousness! If you come to God based on whether you yourself are righteous enough, you will never believe that you are worthy to receive anything. But if you realize that God's kind of righteousness has been freely and eternally given as a gift, you will begin embracing your worthiness before Him! Receive as a gift the *fact* that you are righteous—all day, every day. If you get that, all other things can be added to you.

. . . .

Prayer of Agreement
I believe You, Father, that You have given me Your own righteousness as a pure gift. I choose to quit striving to gain my own righteousness. Instead, I receive the fact that I am always righteous in Jesus. Help me put this truth deep down inside of my heart so that I never doubt it.

God Has a Label
for You

"Blessed be the God and Father, of our Lord Jesus Christ, who has blessed us with every spiritual blessing in the heavenly realms because we are united with Christ."

—Ephesians 1:3

What do you call yourself when no one else is around? Do you say, "I'm righteous. I'm good. I'm approved. I'm a son (or a daughter) of my heavenly Father." Or do you label yourself with other words? "I'm so stupid, I'm so dumb. I'm such a mess-up." Listen, God never labels you in that ugly way. Back in Jesus' day, if you were sick, there was a label given to you by religious peo- ple, "unclean." Sick people were unclean. Lepers were unclean. Even the blind man and the lame man were seen as cursed of God. I can imagine that some of these sick people would say to themselves, "I'm so cursed!" Someone might ask them, "What's your name?" They would answer in despair, "I am Cursed of God." I don't know what labels you have given yourself, or what labels you have accepted from others, but the label that your heavenly Father gives you is, "beloved son/daughter, pleasing to Me." That's what the Father said over Jesus. And the Bible says in 1 John 4:17 that "*as He (Jesus) is, so are we in this world.*" Psalm 33:12 says, *"Blessed (are the people) whose God is the L*ORD*"* God has given you a name: "blessed"!

. . . .

Prayer of Agreement

I believe You, Father, when You call me "blessed." I believe You that You call me "clean" before You, and that what You call "clean," we should never call "unclean." I am the blessed of the Lord. I am Your blessed one today—the successful one, the victorious one—because Your favor rests on me. Jesus, I receive what You say!

Living Fearlessly
in an Age of Terror

"Then the angel said to her, 'Do not be afraid, Mary, for you have found favor with God. And behold, you will conceive in your womb and bring forth a Son, and shall call His name JESUS (Yahweh Saves).'"

—*Luke 1:30–31*

We certainly are living in an age of terror and fear, aren't we? Terror attacks, fear for our country, fear for our children—so much of it is beyond our control. When you are in fear, you cannot enjoy life. Jesus has given us a better way to live. His answer to people in turmoil or sickness or condemnation was to "fear not." His birth was surrounded with "fear not"s. To Zacharias and Joseph, and Mary and the shepherds, the first words were "fear not!" To Jairus whose daughter was sick, to Simon in the boat, to the disciples when He walked on water, Jesus said, "Fear not." Even in the book of Revelation, the first words of Jesus, in Revelation 1:7 are, "Do not be afraid." Jesus, by His life and proclamation, was announcing that the time of fear was over. God is a "fear not" God and He wants you to live a "fear not" life. His perfect love casts out fear. Jesus said, "Abide in that love." When we know that the Father loves us, we know that we will be cared for. When we know that the Father loves us, we know that He is our forgiver and our help in life, and that He is not going to condemn us.

. . . .

Prayer of Agreement

Jesus, I believe You, that I am a part of Your "fear not" kingdom, and that You want me to live boldly in Your love and joy and peace. Today, I exchange my fear for the certainty of Your salvation in all things pertaining to my life. I receive Your word for me today; I will not be afraid.

God Restores
Your Hope

"Now may the God of hope fill you with all joy and peace in believing, that you may abound in hope by the power of the Holy Spirit."

—*Romans 15:13*

Do you need some hope today? Is there a situation in your life for which you just don't see a good resolution? You know, the Bible says in Romans 15:13 that God is the God of hope. He is the origin of all real hope for you. But it's even stronger than that, because the word "hope" in our culture is more like a wish. Hope, to us, doesn't have an ending that is certain. God's hope is a sure and certain expectation of good for your life. You could very well translate the biblical word for "hope" as "expectation." God is not the "God of uncertain

wishing"; He is the "God of good expectation."
He has plans for good. For every devastation and
dead dream, He is convinced that it can be turned
to blessing and good. For every situation that has
an uncertain end, God is convinced that He can
and will bring a positive outcome. Don't box God
in to a specific solution. Let God be God. Agree
with Him on this. Don't give up. God will deliver
good to you.

. . . .

Prayer of Agreement

*Father, I believe what you say about Your
hope for me. Thank You that You abound in
the certain expectation for good regarding
my life. I am convinced that You will resolve
the things that appear unresolvable, and that
Your goodness is ready to manifest.*

You Are Beautiful
to Jesus!

"For by one offering He (Jesus) has perfected forever those who are being sanctified."

—*Hebrews 10:14*

What do you see when you look in the mirror? Are you having a bad hair day, feeling a bit overweight, maybe frustrated with your body? God can help you with those outward things—He really will!—but the source of beauty is found on the inside. God wants you to know how beautiful you are *already* to Him. God is Spirit, and He judges by spirit truth. Jesus said in John 4 that those who come to the Father must come in spirit and in truth. The truth about your spirit is that you are holy and without blame (Ephesians 1:4). You are righteous and perfected forever (Hebrews

10:14). You are His masterpiece (Ephesians 2:10). Can you see yourself that way? In the Song of Solomon, the bride (that's you) says to the groom (that's Jesus): "I am not beautiful to behold. Stay away from me." Jesus responds, in Song of Solomon 4:7, – "No, you are all fair, my love. I see no flaw in you. You are beautiful to Me." That is how Jesus, your Groom, sees you! Many people struggle with the idea that God could see them in such a positive way. We consider ourselves to be ugly before Him. But God is saying to you today, "Stop putting yourself down: You're beautiful to Me." Whatever your body looks like, carry yourself with confidence in the good opinion of Jesus!

. . . .

Prayer of Agreement
Jesus, I will believe what You say about me, that I am beautiful. I choose to believe Your opinion of me above my own. I submit to what You say and gladly rest in Your love for me.

Jesus Delivers You
from Shame

"Then they crucified Him, and divided His garments, casting lots, that it might be fulfilled which was spoken by the prophet, 'They divided My garments among them, and for My clothing they cast lots.'"

—*Matthew 27:35–36*

Do you ever find yourself thinking about some horrible mistake you made, and feeling so much shame about what you did? I mean, you're a believer in Jesus and you know that He's forgiven you, but you have trouble forgiving yourself for the pain you have caused and the shame that your actions have brought. It could have happened a year ago, or ten years ago, or twenty, and yet it never seems to lose its power. Jesus wants you to know that He didn't just bear your guilt for sin on the cross, but He also bore your shame. His stripes were for your healing. His blood was for your forgiveness. His crown of thorns was for your worries, but His nakedness was for your shame. He took your shame off of you and put it on Himself. You must let Him have it. You must see it on Him, then let yourself off the hook. He wanted to take it. Give the shame to Him. Cover yourself, instead, in the love, grace, and approval of your wonderful Savior.

. . . .

Prayer of Agreement

I believe You, Jesus, that You took my sin away from me; and with my sin went my shame. When the memories of my sin come back to me, I choose to take those thoughts captive, releasing them only to Jesus on the cross. The shame is no longer mine to bear. Thank You for loving me so much, Jesus!

Jesus Will Clean
Your Conscience

"Let us therefore come boldly to the throne of grace, that we may obtain mercy and find grace to help in time of need."

—*Hebrews 4:16*

It's nice when you can say, against an accusation, "I am innocent; my conscience is clear. I have a clean conscience." There's a confidence in that, isn't there? Like, that accusation can never stick against you. Do you know that that place of confidence is something Jesus has given you to walk in all the time? The cleansing power of His blood over you is so powerful and thorough that, right now, before God, you can go boldly to Him. That's how thoroughly righteous Jesus has made you. If you are not feeling that way, the Bible says that you need to have your heart sprinkled from an evil conscience (Hebrews 10:22). You need to sprinkle your conscience with the blood of Jesus. An *evil conscience,* by definition, is a conscience that contradicts what God says. An evil conscience contradicts the Gospel. It is anti-Jesus. It is evil. You need to apply the gospel to that conscience. Sprinkle that conscience with His blood! You are clean and innocent. Get your confidence back!

. . . .

Prayer of Agreement

I believe what You say about me, Jesus, that I am forgiven and free of shame! When my conscience begins to condemn me for my past wrongs, and speaks against the righteousness that You gave to me, I choose to believe what You say instead. I am holy and acceptable to You!

God May be
Contradicting You

"If we deny Him, He also will deny us. If we are faithless, He remains faithful; He cannot deny Himself. "

—*2 Timothy 2:12–13*

In Jesus, God says that you are holy and without blame, righteous and worthy of blessings. He calls you His beautiful bride forever, in whom He sees no flaw. That's you all the time, apart from your works. God wants you to embrace what He says about you. If you don't agree with God about your identity, you will never enter the joy that God finds over you. Agree with Him! God is not waiting for you to mess up so that He can "write you off." There's a misunderstood verse in 2 Timothy 2:12 that says, "If we deny Him, He will also deny us." It sounds like Jesus might be ready to forsake a believer if they ever deny Him. But the Greek word for "deny" actually means "to contradict." What this is really saying is, if we contradict what God says over us, God will not change His opinion; He will contradict us! You can contradict God and say that you are just an unworthy, old sinner, but God will never agree with you. He will contradict you and say, "You are My beautiful bride." Believe Him!

. . . .

Prayer of Agreement

I believe what You say about me, Jesus, that I am beloved and accepted, righteous and worthy of blessings. Thank You that, even in my weakest moments, You see me the same! How wonderful You are!

You Are as You
Ought to Be

"The God-setting-things-right that we read about has become Jesus-setting-things-right for us. And not only for us, but for everyone who believes in him."
—*Romans 3:22 MSG*

It's so easy to get into strife with people, isn't it? Whether it's people at work who are difficult to deal with or family members who don't see things like you do, it's easy for relationships to turn sideways. If you're like me, you really want things to be on an even keel with people. And how much worse if you add to that a feeling that you are also sideways with God, feeling like you haven't prayed enough, or gone to church enough, just a sense that things are out of kilter with Him. Hey, those feelings toward God are not serving you the truth. Do you know that *Thayer's Bible Lexicon* defines a righteous person as, "one who is as he ought to be." The Bible says that Jesus has given you righteousness as a gift, apart from the works of the Law. It belongs to you, by gift, apart from whether you do right or wrong! This is the truth; you are *"as you ought to be"* before God. When you understand this, it becomes easier to let go of offense toward other people. It's like getting a fresh start every time you need it during the day. Because we are right with God, we can find new strength to deal with other relationships.

. . . .

Prayer of Agreement

I believe You, Father, when You say that You have set things right between us. This makes me so happy, because I could never get this right by my own efforts. Today, I choose to live in the moment-by-moment reality that I am "as I ought to be" with You and that You are helping me to carry this peace into my other relationships.

Contentment
Belongs to You

"His divine power has given to us all things that pertain to life and godliness, through the knowledge of Him who called us by glory and virtue."

—*2 Peter 1:3*

Are you content? Are you satisfied with your life right now? Are you able to enjoy your life, and enjoy this good day the Lord has made? One of the benefits of the gospel is contentment. Paul wrote in Philippians 4:11, *"I have learned in whatever state I am, to be content."* When you realize that Jesus has eternally reconciled you to the Father, that He is at peace toward you, that you are secure in His love, and that He will never depart from you; when you stop relating to God by the works of the law, and begin relating to Him as sons and daughters, then your striving finally ends. You're done trying to be qualified for His love. You've arrived in it. You abide in it. Here is the place of contentment. You have the greatest prize of all: the love and approval of your Father! In this place of His love, everything else you need is provided for. He gives to you everything that you need for life and godliness! That is what is available to you right now. This is the kingdom of God, and it is within your reach.

. . . .

Prayer of Agreement

I believe You, Father, that You are at peace with me. I believe You, that today I have everything I need because You love me and care for me. For any area in my life where I feel lack, I choose to give this over to Your infinite love for me, and rest in the knowledge that everything I need for life and godliness has been given to me.

Your Life *Matters*

"Are not five sparrows sold for two copper coins? And not one of them is forgotten before God. But the very hairs of your head are all numbered. Do not fear therefore; you are of more value than many sparrows."

—*Luke 12:6–7*

Do you ever wonder how much your life actually matters? Do you question, *Does God really care about me? Among the billions of people on the planet, do I count with God? Do I ever really have His attention?* Jesus wants to convince you that you matter. "The very hairs of your head are all numbered," He said. Can you understand this picture that Jesus wants you to envision? It is the picture of a mother holding her newborn, filled with such love for her baby that she is counting the fingers and toes over and over again. She is loving every detail of her child. God loves you like that, but in even greater detail. He counts the hairs on your head! Can you see yourself in His arms, loving you? You don't have to *do* anything; the baby doesn't do anything; he or she simply is. That's you. Let Him love you. Jesus said He's the shepherd who leaves the ninety-nine in search of the one. You, the one, matter to Him! He is the woman who lost the coin. The woman searched *until* she found that coin. Just so, Jesus searches until He finds you. He will not give up on You. He will not! You are valuable and significant. You don't have to work to get His attention. You have it.

. . . .

Prayer of Agreement

I believe what You say, Jesus, that I matter, and that my life matters, and I perpetually have Your attention. Thank You for caring about my life. I choose to believe that my entire life interests You. Thank You for Your great love for me.

Deliverance from
Depression

"And the ransomed of the LORD shall return and come to Zion with singing, with everlasting joy on their heads. They shall obtain joy and gladness, and sorrow and sighing shall flee away."

—*Isaiah 35:10*

Let me bare my heart a moment with you. For years I suffered from some pretty severe depression, needing medication to help balance out my emotions. I have felt the black clouds come on me. I know the despair of life. I was a pastor for twenty years before I discovered the answer that delivered me from a life of misery. I realized three things: Number one, God was never angry with me, and the sins of my life, from start to finish, were taken off of me by Jesus. Number two, because He was never angry with me, I could believe in His love for me. Why would He *not* love me if my sins were no longer in the way? Number three, my true self was not a depressed person, but a joyful person. In Christ, you *are* a joyful person. Jesus came so that your joy would be full. Whenever I feel a bout of depression come on me, I immediately listen to one of my favorite preachers, who I know will reliably preach the gospel! I believe what is preached, and the black cloud leaves me. I have been completely delivered from depression and medication for eight years now and I'm never going back. Can you hear the hope that He's giving you today? There is an answer.

. . . .

Prayer of Agreement

Jesus, I receive what You say about me, that I am a joyful person. When I feel the black cloud of depression descending upon me, I will hear the gospel again. I will remember that You are never angry with me and that Your love is always the reality from which I find life.

God Believes You
Are a Success

"And suddenly a voice came from heaven, saying, 'This is My beloved Son, in whom I am well pleased.'"

—*Matthew 3:17*

A few years ago I was talking to a man who had been a pastor for forty years. He was now retired and reflecting back on his life. He said to me, "How do I know if I've even been successful?" Isn't that a question many of us ask as we get older? When have we ever done enough to feel like we've had a successful life with God? God has a peculiar answer to that. When Jesus was baptized, the voice from heaven spoke out saying, *"This is My beloved Son in whom I am well pleased."* Think about it! The Father said those words to Jesus before Jesus had done a single thing in ministry. The Father measures success in terms of relationship, not deeds. Jesus related to God as a Son. God related to Jesus as a Father. That is success. The moment you surrendered your life to Jesus and let God love you, you became successful. This means that you are starting out every day from the platform of success. It means that you are ending every day from the platform of success. We need to stop asking the question, "Have I accomplished the will of God for my life?" Start embracing the truth; your life *is* the will of God.

. . . .

Prayer of Agreement
I believe what You say over me, Father, that You are well pleased with me. Thank You that I begin every day from the platform of success in Your eyes.

You Are Delivered
from Hypocrisy

"Woe to you, scribes and Pharisees, hypocrites! For you cleanse the outside of the cup and dish, but inside they are full of extortion and self-indulgence."
—Matthew 23:25

Do you ever feel like a hypocrite, like you want to be holy, but your life just isn't measuring up? Jesus said that this was the issue with the Pharisees. He told us to beware of the leaven of the Pharisees, which is hypocrisy. See, the Pharisees had clean behavior (the outside of the cup was clean), but their hearts were like unclean graveyards. The answer to this hypocrisy is not to "try harder to live cleaner." No, Jesus' answer was to "clean the inside of the cup." He was pointing to the inner man: the thoughts, beliefs, and intentions of the heart. Jesus is the only One who can do this for us, and He does it as a gift. He gives to you the gift of righteousness. Like He said to the woman caught in the act of adultery, He says; "I do not condemn you." When you receive the gift of "no condemnation," a miracle happens in your heart. Your heart is softened toward God, you begin to want to forgive others and your stony heart is replaced with a heart that responds to God and His love for us. Jesus says to you right now, "I do not condemn you." He declares your inner man to be clean and acceptable. And from that place of complete acceptance, your life will change. When the inside is made clean, the outside will soon follow. Receive His "no condemnation."

. . . .

Prayer of Agreement
I believe what You say over me, Father, that I am clean inside and out because of Jesus! I know that as I agree with You about this, my outer behavior will begin to reflect Your righteousness and Your love.

From Servants
to Sons

"And a slave does not abide in the house forever, but a son abides forever."

—*John 8:35*

When Jesus instructed the Jews of His day to call God "Father," He was turning the religious world on its head. In fact, Jesus was introducing a new way to live for a people who saw themselves as servants of God and who were worn out by endless religious duties. Over and over again, Jesus taught the people that their relationship with God was not Master/servant, but was Father/son. A servant is motivated by and lives by the commands that come from a master. A son is motivated by and lives by the love of the family. A servant can't stay in the house forever, only a son. Now reflect on how you live your life before God. If you see yourself primarily as the servant of the Lord, trying to keep all His commands, you will never enter His rest. You will always be trying to earn your place in the kingdom by your efforts. But the kingdom doesn't come by effort; it comes by inheritance, by gift, by love. That's sonship! That is such a higher position than servant, and it leads to a restful life in His family.

. . . .

Prayer of Agreement

I believe what You say, Father, that I am a son and not a servant. I choose to live by Your love for me. Thank You for teaching me more and more how to rest in the love of Your family.

God's Good *Plan*

"For our citizenship is in heaven, from which we also eagerly wait for the Savior, the Lord Jesus Christ."

—*Philippians 3:20*

"And now, Lord, what do I wait for? My hope is in You."

—*Psalm 39:7*

Every four years in the United States, there is a potential change in political power. And every time one political party replaces another, half of our population's anxiety level goes through the roof. People believe that their future looks bleak or bright, depending on what party is in power. I do not want to minimize the effect that a president's decisions can have on us all, but the fact is that God is not dependent on a particular party being in power in order to bless us or for our personal ministries to prosper. God is able to bless us no matter who is in office. And we are able to love no matter who is in office. It's faith that really matters. God has a good plan for your life. *"I know the thoughts that I think toward you, says the Lord, thoughts of peace and a hope"* (Jeremiah 29:11). That promise is not contingent upon your candidate winning an election. It is a simple promise of God, that His goodness, prosperity, and hope will manifest in your life. He never ceases to be your loving, providing Father. Rest in that.

. . . .

Prayer of Agreement
I believe what You say, Father, that I am secure and provided for in all political environments. Thank You that Your kingdom undergirds my life and ministry, and that I am well cared for.

Is God Angry with our Country?

"Righteousness exalts a nation, but sin is a reproach to any people."

—*Proverbs 14:34*

Are you anxious for our nation today? Do you wonder about God's wrath toward us as a people? We need to get this right: God's posture is not one of wrath or judgment. Jesus took all that upon himself. *"God was in Christ reconciling the world to Himself, not imputing their trespasses to them, and has committed to us the word of reconciliation"* (2 Corinthians 5:19). In the New Covenant, Jesus showed us the Father's heart. You know the verse —John 3:16 – *"For God so hated this world that . . ."* Oh, is that wrong? "For God was so exasperated with this world . . . er . . . He was so frustrated

. . . He was so angry. . . " No. *"For God so loved the world."* He loves us. He's not ready to thump us. As a country, we can make bad decisions all day long that might ruin the economy or foster injustice or make things hard for people. The results of those decisions could really be bad. But God's heart is to bless us through His love. You can pray with confidence today in God's love for us and release the Kingdom of God over us as a people. Release protection, prosperity, health, and goodness over our country. What an awesome privilege, that we get to do this today!

. . . .

Prayer of Agreement

Jesus, I believe what You say, that the Father loves us and, in that love, wants to bless us. I speak out blessing over my country: health, righteous laws, prosperity, wisdom, love, peace, and joy!

God's Goodness
Leads to Repentance

"By this all will know that you are My disciples, if you have love for one another."

—*John 13:35*

With famines, wars, and injustices that decimate peaceful living, we all want the world to improve in so many ways. Do you know that God's way to effect massive change is by convincing one heart at a time of how much He loves us? The Bible says in Romans 2:4, *"Or do you despise the riches of His goodness, forbearance, and longsuffering, not knowing that the goodness of God leads you to repentance?"* God changes one heart at a time by showing forth His goodness and by proving out His love to people—sinning people, ungodly people. We can enter into God's work of transformation when we speak and show forth His goodness and love to people, introducing them to the real Jesus. Threats of judgment and wrath aren't going to make a difference. Prophecies of impending doom are not from the Lord; Jesus said that people who want to call down fire "do not know what manner of spirit [they] are of" (Luke 9:55). But you and I will effect change when we stay in the love of God, and show forth that love, and tell people where that love came from: the Lord Jesus Christ!

. . . .

Prayer of Agreement

Father, I believe what You say, that Your goodness and love will lead people to change their minds about You and embrace Jesus. Thank You that Your goodness and love are inside of me and are part of my real identity. Thank You for courage to release this into the world around me!

God Calls You to
Reign and Rule

"Behold, I give you the authority to trample on serpents and scorpions, and over all the power of the enemy, and nothing shall by any means hurt you."

—*Luke 10:19*

God told us in Genesis 1:26–28 to take dominion over this earth. You were created to be a person who reigns and rules. That doesn't mean that we are to give orders to other people. It means that we exercise our authority over life situations and over this earth. We speak out healing over people and over ourselves. We walk in peace, love, and joy, setting the atmosphere of a room by our presence. That confidence and authority is not something you simply psyche yourself up for; it's something you live out of. When you know that you are eternally forgiven, loved, favored, accepted, worthy, and holy (all the things Jesus has given to you as a gift) the authority will show up in your very presence. The joy within you will spill out. The love within you will spill out. The goodness and healing and peace within you will spill out. Romans 5:17 says that through the abundance of grace and the gift of righteousness, we reign in life through Jesus Christ. Abundance of grace! Receive this abundance and change your world.

. . . .

Prayer of Agreement

Jesus, I believe what You say over me, that I have received authority from You to change the world around me. I receive the super-abundance of grace for my life and the pure gift of Your righteousness within me. And from that place of oneness with You, I set out to reign in life today, by the leading of Your Holy Spirit!

Understand the
Love of God

"Beloved, let us love one another, for love is of God; and everyone who loves is born of God and knows God. He who does not love does not know God, for God is love."

—1 John 4:7–8

You were wired by God to partake of His love. The Bible says, "God is love." Love is within the very being of God. And Jesus teaches us to abide in His love. First Corinthians 13, the famous love chapter, is a description of God's kind of love. Remember? Love is patient, love is kind, love keeps no record of wrongdoing. This is exactly how God loves you! In fact, you could replace the word "love" with the word "God." God is patient and kind; God does not envy; God is not provoked (wow, you can't provoke God!); God keeps no record of wrongs done; God bears all things, believes all things, hopes all things, endures all things. God never fails. That whole chapter is a description, at its heart, of how God loves us. And it begins this way: *"though I have the gift of prophecy...and though I have all faith, so that I could remove mountains, but have not love, I am nothing."* You can be religious, have prophetic words, speak in tongues, and do miracles, but if you never learn to abide in God's love for you, you are nothing. You miss who you really are! Receive His love and come into your true self!

. . . .

Prayer of Agreement
I believe what You say, Father, that You are love and that I am meant to live in that love. I reject a life of wondering whether or not You love me. I receive and abide in Your love. And I will live out of that love and accept it as my true identity, because I am made in Your image.

Stop Bargaining
with God

"He who did not spare His own Son, but delivered Him up for us all, how shall He not with Him also freely give us all things?"

—*Romans 8:32*

A lot of people, when they're at a place of desperation, begin to bargain with God: "God, if You heal me, I'll be able to serve You better: God, if You get me out of this financial bind, I can give so much more to the Church." Bargaining with God for a blessing is the position of a servant to a master. A servant trades extra duties to get a small sliver of favor. In Jesus, you are no longer servants, but sons. Think of how absurd it would be if your child were sick with cancer and came begging to you, "Please, Mom, please heal me and I promise I will clean the house for you every day." The mother's heart would break at hearing that. She would say, "Stop! I love and heal you because you're my daughter, not because you serve me." That's how God feels. He who gave us His own Son, will He not give us all things with Him? If God withholds any good thing from us, it means that He prizes that thing more than He prizes His own Son. Impossible! As it would be with any good mother or father, *"it is [His] good pleasure to give you the kingdom"* (Luke 12:32). Just ask, by His love.

. . . .

Prayer of Agreement

I believe what You say, Jesus, that the Father delights in giving me good things. Thank You, Father, that You are not withholding any good thing from me. I am not going to bargain with You anymore! I will trust in the strength of Your love for me. Today, I receive good things from You, based on my sonship.

God Will Never
Leave You

Let your conduct be without covetousness; be content with such things as you have. For He Himself has said, 'I will never leave you nor forsake you.'"
—*Hebrews 13:5*

One of the low-level fears of so many believers is the fear that they may do something to separate themselves from God forever. But in Jesus, God says, "I will never leave you nor forsake you." Think about it. The words "leave you" can be temporary; I can leave and I can come back. But "forsaking you" is permanent. It's God throwing up His hands and saying about you, "I give up on you." In the New Covenant, God promises to *never* temporarily leave you. He never pops in and out of fellowship with you. He's not there when you are good, but then and out of fellowship with you when you sin. No, He never leaves you *and* He never forsakes you. He never gets to a place where He says about you, "I've had it with this woman. I give up." Think about it, in Jesus you have become the Father's child. You are part of His household forever. Nothing can snatch you from His hand. How many ways does He need to say it? This is the promise about you; "I will *never* leave you nor forsake you." End of story.

. . . .

Prayer of Agreement

Father, I believe what You say to me, that You will never leave me and You will never forsake me. I establish my heart in this truth. And today, I will walk without fear of your rejection, no matter what!

You Are More Than
You Think

"When I consider Your heavens, the work of Your fingers, the moon and the stars, which You have ordained, what is man that You are mindful of him, and the son of man that You visit him? For You have made him a little lower than the angels*, and You have crowned him with glory and honor."

—*Psalm 8:3-5*

*the Hebrew word here is "Elohim," most often translated as "God"

An abusive relationship is one in which the victim is made to feel less than human, smaller and of less value than they really are. Our wrong beliefs can become like an abusive spouse, diminishing our value by calling us "worms" or unworthy sinners. The Bible says just the opposite; it says you are made in the image and likeness of God. You are the God-kind, made to partake of His fellowship, made to be His holy temple that He will inhabit forever. Jesus restored you permanently to that position. Don't think of yourself any less than the spotless, perfect Bride of Christ. What lengths the Father has gone in His love to save you! How valuable must you be! Cry out with the psalmist, *"What is man that though art mindful of him?"* He was not saying, *"Oh, what a terrible creature I am! I wonder why You pay me any attention at all?"* Just the opposite! The psalmist looked at the favor and attention God was paying him, how the entire world was created for humanity, and he cried out, "What is man! *What must we be!* . . . that God would go to such lengths!" Enjoy the truth of who He created you to be!

. . . .

Prayer of Agreement

I believe what You say about me, Father, that I am made in Your image! I choose to look to the Rock from which I was hewn, and You are that Rock! Thank You, Father, that You created me special.

The "Right Now" God

"And which of you by worrying can add one cubit to his stature? If you then are not able to do the least, why are you anxious for the rest?"

—*Luke 12:25–26*

Is your mind on yesterday, on things you may regret? Or is your mind on the future and things you may be worried about for tomorrow? The two things that rob us of enjoying today are the regrets of yesterday and the worries of tomorrow. Isn't it telling that the name of God as revealed to Moses was *Yahweh*, which means, "I am." I am, as in "present tense." "I am the eternally present tense One." God wants you to enjoy Him in the right now. Jesus lived that way. Jesus didn't regret the things He did yesterday. And He didn't worry about what was coming tomorrow. He lived, fully present, in the right now, enjoying the love that the Father had for Him at every moment. That's how we are to live. Can you take a moment to be fully present with God right now? Can you see that yesterday is gone, and forgiveness has cleansed you of every mistake? Can you see that tomorrow's worries are in the hands of your loving Father? Trade in your yesterdays and tomorrows for the experience of God's love and joy in the right now.

. . . .

Prayer of Agreement

I believe You, Father, that You are I Am, the God of the right now. Thank You that You are fully present with me, even when my mind is on yesterday or tomorrow. Thank You for the eternal invitation to join You in the right now of my life, and receive Your rest and love and joy!

Something Good Is
Going to Happen to You!

"Now to Him who is able to do exceedingly abundantly
above all that we ask or think, according to the power
that works in us, to Him be glory in the church by Christ
Jesus to all generations, forever and ever."

—*Ephesians 3:20-21*

Christians are all about giving thanks. Philippians
4:6 says, *"Be anxious for nothing, but in everything,
by prayer and petition, with thanksgiving, present your requests to God."* The reason we ask the
Father *"with thanksgiving"* is because we know
that He always hears our prayers, and He always
says "yes" to His goodness being poured out on
our lives. Maybe the exact answer won't come
about in the way we think it should, but we can
know that He will bless us with goodness that is

beyond what we could ask or think. Think about that! God always imagines a much better solution for us than we are capable of coming up with ourselves! That's how good He is! When we offer prayer *"with thanksgiving,"* it's because we know that something good is coming, even better than what we asked! When we believe this, we don't have to manufacture our thanksgiving toward God. We don't have to pretend to be thankful. But when we're persuaded of His goodness, we will give thanks, because we'll know that something good is about to happen. Something good is going to happen to you today!

. . . .

Prayer of Agreement

I believe You, Father, that something very good is coming to me at every request. In fact, my heart is so excited at the potential of what will manifest, that a thankfulness arises in me before I even see the results! Thank You that I can count on Your great love for me!

Jesus Is Your
Jubilee Freedom

"The Spirit of the LORD is upon Me, because He has anointed Me to preach the gospel to the poor; He has sent Me to heal the brokenhearted, to proclaim liberty to the captives and recovery of sight to the blind, to set at liberty those who are oppressed; to proclaim the acceptable year of the Lord... And He began to say to them, 'Today this Scripture is fulfilled in your hearing.'"

—*Luke 4:18-21*

We have so many things to be thankful for, don't we—our family, our jobs, our places to live? All these things are real blessings from the Father. But Jesus came to add a whole other dimension of goodness and blessing to us, something that nobody had had before, even people who were blessed mightily with family and job and home. Jesus says that He came "to proclaim the acceptable year of the LORD." That is a reference to the year of Jubilee in Israel! The year of Jubilee was the year when all debt was forgiven and all land was returned to families. It is a picture of what Jesus has truly done for you. He has permanently forgiven all your debt to God. The sin debt of your entire life is "paid in full"! Additionally, Jesus has given you back your inheritance as a child of God. The promised land was a symbol of this inheritance. In the Year of Jubilee, every family got their land back! Then Jesus said, *"This is fulfilled in your hearing."* You receive it by hearing and believing. Believe it today!

. . . .

Prayer of Agreement

Jesus, I believe what You say about me, that my sin debt is paid in full forever and that my inheritance as a son/daughter of God is returned to me. I receive my inheritance as a gift, and my heart rejoices over what You've done for me. Thank You, Jesus!

Receive as a Child
Receives

"Assuredly, I say to you, whoever does not receive the kingdom of God as a little child will by no means enter it."

—*Luke 18:17*

Jesus said, *"It is your Father's good pleasure to give you the kingdom"* (Luke 12:32). God loves to give good things to His kids. We should expect His goodness to manifest and receive it with joy. That's a different way to live than the way of the world. The world is in "take mode." Take what you want. Take what belongs to you. It's all about *your ability* to get. The Old Covenant was based on this idea. Jesus said, *"From the days of John the Baptist until now the kingdom of heaven suffers violence, and the violent take it by force"* (Matthew 11:12).

84

The New Covenant doesn't work that way. In the New Covenant, Jesus says, anyone who doesn't *"receive the kingdom of God as a little child will by no means enter it."* It's receiving, not taking. A little child has no ability to take from her parents. She can only receive what is given. How wonderful! This puts all the burden on the parent. It's not up to us! In taking, you make it happen. In receiving, God makes it happen, and you just receive what He's done. Hold your hands out and receive what you need today from your good, good Father.

. . . .

Prayer of Agreement

I believe You, Father, that I don't have to try to forcibly take the blessings of Your kingdom, but that You freely offer them to me. I come to You as a little child ready to receive, and I allow You to be the One who gets Your kingdom to me.

Holiday *Loneliness*

*"How precious also are Your thoughts to me, O God!
How great is the sum of them! If I should count
them, they would be more in number than the sand."*
—Psalm 139:17–18

Holidays and birthdays can be lonely times for
some people who don't have friends or family
nearby. It can make a person feel insignificant,
even forgotten, in the world. Please don't let that
negative emotion sit in the driver's seat of your
thinking. A sense of "forgotten-ness" is not the
truth about your situation. Why not let the Father
remind you of how loved you are? He said, "I love
you with an everlasting love (Jeremiah 31:3). I
have not forgotten you; I could never do that. Can
a mother forget her nursing baby? Even if that
were possible, I could never forget you (Isaiah
49:15). You are My special one. I knew you be-

fore you were born (Jeremiah 1:5); My thoughts toward you were as numerous as the sand on the shore when you were in the womb, and every one of them was a thought of love (Psalm 139:17–18). You were My dream. And the day you were born was the day My dream came true. I love you. I'm not holding your sins against you (2 Corinthians 5:19); My Son took all your sin away, so you can receive all My love. I invite you to believe this. To rest in this. To find your strength in My love for you."

. . . .

Prayer of Agreement
I believe what You say over me, Father, that I am always remembered by You. Thank You that You call me valuable and beloved. I set my mind on this truth, and turn my mind from the lie that I could ever be forgotten. It's such a joy to be loved so much by You!

You Can Trust
Your Heart

"My sheep hear My voice, and I know them, and they follow Me."

—*John 10:27*

Do you ever wish that you could hear God's voice better?   I mean, do you wish that you could hear God speak to you clearly so that you could make right decisions and know that you are following Jesus? Jesus said, *"My sheep hear My voice."* Do you hear the certainty in these words? This is not a description of a person striving to hear Him. It's a simple statement of fact; His sheep hear His voice. You hear Jesus' voice. But Jesus is speaking to you on the deepest level of communication, the heart level. Jesus said, "Abide in Me; abide in My love." To abide means "to remain in," or "to pitch a tent in." You cannot hear Him apart from abiding in His love. God only broadcasts on the love channel. In that place, He will give you the desires of your heart. In other words, He will put things in your heart that you *want* to do. What is your heart saying? That's the voice of Jesus. Jesus said, "Abide in Me." Do that. Abide in Him and His love for you, and then ask yourself, "What is in my heart.'" You are hearing Jesus' voice. Satan will teach you not to trust your heart. But God's love has replaced your stony heart with a heart that responds to Him. In His love, ask yourself, What is my heart saying? Follow that voice. It's Jesus.

. . . .

Prayer of Agreement

I believe You, Jesus, that I hear Your voice and follow You. Thank You for speaking so clearly to my heart and for giving me desires that are straight from You. Help me to trust my heart, and trust what You're saying to me. Thank You for loving me so much that You speak to me!

You Become What
You Believe

"A good man out of the good treasure of his heart*
brings forth good things, and an evil man out of the
evil treasure brings forth evil things."

—*Matthew 12:35*

*[definition of heart – the place of belief in a person]

What do you believe about yourself? Do you
see yourself as a short-tempered man? Do you
judge yourself to be a failure, an unlovable one,
someone full of lust, or greed, or impatience? The
perpetual sinner who can't break the cycle? The
Bible says, *"As a man thinks in his heart, so is he"*
(Proverbs 23:7). In other words, the you that you
think you are is the you that will manifest in your
life. How important it is to see yourself as God
sees you! God is not seeing or judging you after

the flesh. But God sees you as a new creation in His Son, one spirit with Jesus. It's not you who lives, but Christ who lives in you. The truth about your identity is found in 1 John 4:17: *"As He is, so are we in this world."* As Jesus is, so are we in this world. We are as Jesus is right now, in this world. That's the real you, all the time. Holy, without blame, healthy, prosperous, joyful, peaceful. That's the real you! If you believe that, then that is what will begin to manifest in your life.

. . . .

Prayer of Agreement

I believe You, Jesus, that I am exactly like You in my spirit, because I am joined to You. I receive this as the real me. Thank You for breaking me free from wrong thinking about myself that keeps me locked in sin and defeat. I believe what You say.

Understanding the
Wrath of God

"For the wrath of God is revealed from heaven against all ungodliness and unrighteousness of men, who suppress the truth in unrighteousness."

—Romans 1:18

The "wrath of God" in the New Testament is often misunderstood by believers. Because God is love, even His wrath must be understood in light of His loving passion for humanity. When do we see Jesus exhibiting wrath? One could argue that the only time Jesus exhibited wrath was when He cleansed the Temple. In that day, the religious leaders had allowed money changers, who would change coins into the acceptable currency of the Temple, and animal sellers, who would gladly sell you a preapproved sacrificial animal, to operate in the Outer Court. Imagine the noise, the foul odor of excrement, and the price gouging that was going on. All of these things were impediments to the worshipers who only wanted access to God. Jesus made a whip and drove them all out. "Then He taught, saying to them, 'Is it not written, "My house shall be called a house of prayer for all nations"? But you have made it a "den of thieves"'" (Mark 11:17). Can you envision the anger of the Lord coming against all of these impediments to intimacy with the Father? This is the love-wrath of God that burns against anything that comes between Himself and His people. What inhibits your sense of intimacy with the Father? Is it condemnation, or guilt, or fear? God wants to drive out all those things that get in the way. That's how much He loves you.

. . . .

Prayer of Agreement

Father, I will believe what Jesus says about You, that Your wrath is not hanging over me, ready to destroy me. Thank You that I can be at rest in Your love, because Your perfect love casts out fear of judgment. I receive Your love for me!

Confusing Good
and Bad

"Fear not, for I am with you; be not dismayed, for I am your God. I will strengthen you, yes, I will help you, I will uphold you with My righteous right hand."
—Isaiah 41:10

If you've ever experienced tragedy in your life, you know how hollow the words "everything happens for a reason" really are. My niece was molested for a reason? My friend was murdered for a reason? Children are starving in third world countries for a reason? What we're really saying by that is that God is somehow in control and pulling the strings. Does that even make sense in light of God's re-vealed goodness and love? It doesn't. The truth is that God gave dominion of the earth to human beings. And fallen human beings can commit into horrible evil, evil with which God, *in no way*, agrees. We are misrepresenting God when we say that God is behind all this. How are you going to recognize how good God really is if you are attributing tragedy to Him? The Bible says, "*Woe to them who call evil good and good evil*" (Isaiah 5:20)! Alas to you! God is only good. And you can count on His goodness. Jesus is not breaking the legs of His little sheep to keep them close to Him (good grief!). God is good, all the time.

. . . .

Prayer of Agreement

I believe what You say, Father, that You are the fount of every blessing, not the source of my troubles. I reject every lie that says that You bring calamity on me. I receive the truth of Your goodness. Thank You that I can count on Your goodness toward me!

You Live from
Your Belief

"For if our heart condemns us, God is greater than our heart, and knows all things."

—1 John 3:20

Some people think that God's requirement of faith is peculiar, as though our relationship with God is the only relationship that requires this peculiar thing called "faith." But the truth is that the entirety of your life is lived out of your belief. We were created to function on belief. For instance, my wife truly loves me and tells me so often. Her heart is full of love for me. But if I don't *believe* that she loves me, I will never feel loved. It's my belief in her love that causes me to experience it! It is exactly the same with God. God loves you, truly. But if you don't believe it, you will never feel loved by Him. If you believe in your condemnation, or believe in your shaky position before Him, or believe in your guilt before Him, you will live out of those beliefs. In other words, you will not experience His great love for you. Your unbelief in His love has not changed His heart of love for you, only your ability to receive it. Until you know that you are eternally forgiven and accepted, apart from good or bad behavior, you will never be able to fully receive the love of the Father for you. Let Jesus persuade your heart to believe in the love of God!

. . . .

Prayer of Agreement
Father, I believe what You say about Yourself,
that You love with an everlasting love. Thank
You for continually persuading my heart to
believe in Your love for me.

Jesus Wants You to
Enter His Rest

"Are you tired? Worn out? Burned out on religion? Come to me. Get away with me and you'll recover your life. I'll show you how to take a real rest."
—*Matthew 11:28* MSG

Jesus said to the Jews of His day, *"Come to Me, all you who labor and are heavy laden, and I will give you rest."* He was inviting them into a different way to live with God, a way that was not about rule keeping or working hard to maintain some level of acceptability. *That* way of living with God wore people out. God does not want to wear us out! That's what the devil wants! Jesus called the devil the "evil one." That word for "evil" in the Greek is *poneros*. It means, and I quote *Thayer's Lexicon* "full of labors, annoyances, hardships,

pressed and harassed by labors, bringing toils."
The definition of evil is "full of labors"! Jesus is
referring to the system of the devil that many
religious people cling to. That system sounds like
this, "We will work, work, work, to get right and
stay right with God. We will burn out for God."
That is an evil system; it is anti-Christ because it
makes the work of Jesus to mean nothing. Jesus did
the work for you. Believe it, and enter into His rest.

. . . .

Prayer of Agreement

*I believe You, Jesus, that You want me to
enter a restful life with You. When I start
striving with You and begin living again out
of the lie that You and I are not at peace, help
me hear Your promptings to re-embrace the
truth that You came to give me rest.*

Deliverance from
Persistent Sins

"Their sins and their lawless deeds I will remember no more."

—*Hebrews 10:17*

Jesus has forgiven us, amen? But what do we do about those persistent sins in our lives that we keep coming back to, the ones that we have not yet been able to find victory over? First of all, it's important to remember in such times that those sins, just like all the others, have been taken away by Jesus. He is not dealing with you, ever, according to your iniquities (Psalm 103:10). You can rest in that. Second, the truth about our persistent sins is that they probably have their origins in some very deep woundedness. Jesus is intent on healing up these wounded areas of our hearts, but it often takes time. Know this: Jesus is much more persistent than your sins. He is always at work in you, healing your heart. The remedy for healing up your heart is not to feel the weight of condemnation and be hard on yourself; it's to abide in the complete love and acceptance of Jesus. Our hearts are only healed in the atmosphere of love. In time, these sins will fall off of you as your heart is persuaded of your new identity. And until then, when you fall, just go straight to Jesus. Thank Him that you are already totally forgiven, and receive His perfect love anew.

. . . .

Prayer of Agreement

I believe what You say, Jesus, that I am a new creation in You right now. Thank You that Your love is healing my mind and emotions, and I am free in You to live an upright life. How wonderful You are to me!

Maturing in *Christ*

*"And he said: 'Truly I tell you, unless you change
and become like little children, you will never enter
the kingdom of heaven.'"*

—*Matthew 18:2-3* NIV

"When you pray, say, 'Father.'"

—*Luke 11:2*

Sometimes, we are our own worst critics, aren't
we—especially when it comes to the things we
want to do for God? Maybe we felt led to pray for
someone, but didn't do it. Or perhaps we felt a
word of encouragement rise up for someone, but
we got intimidated and ended up not speaking it
out. Or maybe we *did* say something, but it just
didn't come out exactly right. You know, the Holy
Spirit is such a patient teacher. He knows us thoroughly, and He is not disappointed. Jesus said that
we need to receive the Kingdom as little children.

The responsibility for raising little children is on the parent, not on the child. The parent doesn't get frustrated or angry if the child doesn't learn to walk the first time he stands up. No, the child stands, takes a faulty step, and falls down. The parent is delighted at the progress, and then sets the child up again. On and on. That's how it works. The Father is proud of you for your belief in Jesus. And every time you speak out or do something that springs from His life within you, however imperfect your words or actions might be, there is joy, because you are coming into your true identity.

. . . .

Prayer of Agreement

Father, I believe what You say over me, that I am an accepted child, and I choose to see myself this way before You. I let go of my perfectionism and put myself under Your love, which always accepts me.

The Family Picture
Shows What God Is Like

"For you did not receive the spirit of bondage again to fear, but you received the Spirit of adoption by whom we cry out, 'Abba, Father.'"

—Romans 8:15

The family unit is so important to God! He designed us to thrive in families and to understand them, because families are His picture of how God deals with people. Jesus told us to call God "Father." That's family. We are given the Spirit of adoption as sons. That's family. Jesus is our groom, and we are His bride. Family. Fellow believers are brothers and sisters. It's all family! There is a point to this: The family shows forth how God relates to us. He told us to think about Him in terms of family! If you want to know how God thinks about you, run your thinking through the family paradigm. Does the father put the son's hand on a hot stove to teach him a lesson? No. Never. Then God your Father would never harm you to teach you a lesson. Does a father un-adopt a son because he misbehaves? No. Never. Then God would never un-adopt you. The central revelation of the Holy Spirit within you is for you to cry out in realization, "Abba, Father!" "God is my Father!" "I am His son!" "I am His daughter!" If your theology doesn't fit the family, it's not what God is like.

. . . .

Prayer of Agreement

I believe what You say, Father, that I am a permanent part of Your family! Thank You for Your promises that make me feel secure as Your child. And thank You for my human family, that I can reflect out to them the exquisite love with which You first loved me.

Do You Love God *Enough?*

"In this is love, not that we loved God, but that He loved us and sent His Son to be the propitiation for our sins."

—*1 John 4:10*

"We love Him because He first loved us."

—*1 John 4:19*

Do you ever wonder if you love God enough? I always used to wonder about my own love for God, or really, my lack of love for Him. I desperately wanted to love Him. I knew the right answer to the question, "Do you love God?" I would always say "yes." But the truth is, I felt tremendous guilt and worry that I didn't love God more. I would look around in worship at people who appeared to be truly in love with Him, and I would wonder,

"Why don't I love Him that way? What's wrong with me?" Do you ever have those thoughts? If so, I want you to hear your Father say to you, "Don't worry so much about loving Me. What's most important is that you begin to believe that I love you." You see, you can't love God at all until you receive His love for you, the love that never departs from you because "God is love." His love is always the "first love." Return to your first love. Believe in His eternal, unchanging love for you.

. . . .

Prayer of Agreement

I believe what You say to me, Father, that Your love for me is always first. Today, I return to my first love, Your unchanging love for me. I believe You, Father. You love me.

You Really Are
Flawless

"For by one offering He has perfected forever those who are being sanctified."

—*Hebrews 10:14*

I know many believers who live every day with a low-level sense of condemnation before God. They believe they are striving with their "old man" (the sinner part of them that is at enmity with God), letting the old man speak to them about how they should think about God and themselves. Receive the truth: That old man was crucified with Christ. It is dead. The deeds of that old man have no more claim on your position before God than a dead, man would have. We're not trying to prop that old Adam up with righteous acts. He is dead and we are completely new creations of innocence. Christ did not come to justify our old man; He came to put him to death. He has divorced you from the Old Adam, and Jesus has become one with your spirit. The Bible says, Those who believe are "One Spirit with Him" (1 Corinthians 6:17). Righteousness has been joined to you in Jesus! You are a just person in Christ. Jesus said that a just person has no need for repentance. We need to stop seeing ourselves after the flesh. You are righteous; believe in Christ's work. The cross has made you flawless. Let go of condemnation.

. . . .

Prayer of Agreement

I believe what You say about me, Jesus, that the "old man" in me is dead and has no say in the relationship between You and me. I hold on to the fact that You have joined yourself to me forever. Thank You for my new life in You!

What Do You Want
for Your Birthday?

"Peace I leave with you, My peace I give to you; not as the world gives do I give to you. Let not your heart be troubled, neither let it be afraid."

—*John 14:27*

What do you want for your birthday this year? Any ideas? You know, as I get older, I want fewer and fewer material things. I want more and more of the things that can't be purchased at a store. In fact, the sweetest thing for me is to sit in front of my fireplace or on my back porch and receive the love and peace that belongs to me as a son of God. The moment Jesus was born and God took on human flesh, things changed on the earth. When Jesus was born, the angels announced to the shepherds, *"Peace, goodwill toward men"* (Luke 2:14).

Peace toward men. It was directional. It was from heaven, from God, toward men. When Jesus rose from the dead, His first word to the disciples was "peace." Peace to you. He gave to us His peace. You can be at peace right now by entering His peace. See Him at peace over you. Enter into *that* peace. The work is finished. *"God was in Christ reconciling the world to Himself, not imputing their trespasses to them"* (2Corinthians 5:19). Would you believe that God is reconciled toward you all the time? All the time! This year, on your birthday, when the day is done and you're a year older, take a minute to just sit before God and enjoy His perfect peace toward you.

. . . .

Prayer of Agreement

Father, I believe what You say, that You are at peace toward me right now. In every situation today, I will see You at peace toward me. Thank You for helping me enter Your peace.

God's Gift of *Life*

"For God so loved the world that He gave His only begotten Son, that whoever believes in Him should not perish but have everlasting life."

—*John 3:16*

The greatest gift that anyone can ever receive from the Father is the gift of His very life. Jesus said, "I am the life" (John 14:6). In fact, this is the source of everything else that the Father has for you. And He desires, above all else, to give you His life. This is the gospel. In the end, the gospel isn't about embracing a doctrine or idea; it's about embracing the very life of Jesus. It's about receiving His life inside of you, which is eternal life. Eternal life is God's own quality of life. God's quality of life is not found in the material things of this world. But receiving eternal life is experiencing His love for you, His peace over you, His joy over you, His forgiveness over you, His acceptance of you. These are the things that the Father *wants* you to experience. He "so loved" you. Such is His love that Jesus would come in human flesh and "die your sins away" on the cross, so that you could experience union with the life of God. The material things of the world (the things that you could possess apart from Jesus' death and resurrection) may be necessary for life on this earth, but the presence or absence of these things are no indication of how blessed you are. No, you are blessed because of the eternal life of God that inhabits you, given as a sheer gift.

. . . .

Prayer of Agreement

Father, I believe what Jesus said about You, that Your great love for me has removed all separation between us. I believe in You and the gift that You have given me in Jesus. Today I will be conscious of Your life of love and joy that inhabits me.

What Do You Expect
to Receive from God?

"And the Word became flesh and dwelt among us, and we beheld His glory, the glory as of the only begotten of the Father, full of grace and truth . . . and of His fullness we have all received, and grace for grace."

—*John 1:14, 16*

What are you expecting to receive from God today? When you look back on your behavior the last few days, or the last few months, or even the last few years, do you feel like maybe you should expect to receive a bit of judgment from God? Maybe you think God is tired of the fact that you still haven't learned a particular life lesson, and so you conclude that He is not going to bless you in abundance. In fact, He may mete out a bit of anger your way. Our feelings (our sense of self-condemnation) would lead us to believe that God wouldn't really want to bless us mightily. But the above scripture testifies to just the opposite. Jesus was *"full of grace and truth."* Think about that; He is full of grace (unmerited favor toward you) and truth (He sees things as they really are). But what do we receive from Him? Grace upon grace. We receive from Jesus one dose of grace upon another. We receive from His fullness! To be "full" means there is no room for anything else. Jesus is "full" of grace toward you. Believe that this is true for you! Reject your feeling of condemnation. You received His grace yesterday. What does He have for you today? More grace! Grace upon grace, upon grace, upon grace.

. . . .

Prayer of Agreement

Jesus, I believe what Your Word says about You, that You are full of grace and truth. I thank You that You want me to receive of Your fullness today, grace upon grace. You are so good to me!

God's Spirit Is Convicting You of Righteousness

"And when He [the Holy Spirit] has come, He will
convict the world of sin, and of righteousness, and
of judgment: of sin, because they do not believe in
Me; of righteousness, because I go to My Father and
you see Me no more; of judgment, because the ruler
of this world is judged."   —John 16:8-11

Many people slander the Spirit of God and den-
igrate Him to the position of "Divine Nag." He is,
they believe, the one who convicts us of our sinful
behavior. He is like the spouse who follows us
around the room waiting for us to do something
wrong, and the moment we say or do or even
think something that isn't in perfect agreement
with righteousness, He is all over us, convicting
us until we come to proper repentance. This is an
abhorrent lie. If taken seriously, this belief will
push you further and further away from God in

your mind and drive a sensitive person to religious insanity. The Bible does not say that the Holy Spirit convicts believers of sin. Jesus said that the Spirit would convict the unbelieving world of one sin, the sin of unbelief. Jesus went on to say that the role of the Holy Spirit was to be a comforter to us, and that He would "convict" (or "convince") believers of their righteousness! We need this ministry of the Spirit, because Jesus Himself is not walking on the earth to speak this into us. We need this ministry of the Spirit, because without it our own consciences will condemn us and make us feel unworthy of fellowship with God and unworthy of blessings. Listen to the Spirit within you. He is bearing witness to the power of Jesus' blood. You have been eternally cleansed. You have been given the gift of righteousness as a gift. You are acceptable today to the Father!

. . . .

Prayer of Agreement
Jesus, I believe what You said about the Holy Spirit, that He convicts me of my righteousness! Thank You that You always see me acceptable and worthy of blessings. Today, I agree with the Holy Spirit, that I am righteous, just like You!

117

God Is a Blessing
God

"The LORD bless you and keep you; The LORD make His face shine upon you, and be gracious to you; the LORD lift up His countenance upon you, and give you peace."

—*Number 6:24-26*

God is going to bless you today! I can say that with confidence, because God is a blessing God and not a cursing God. Any cursings you can find in the Old Testament were the result of unrighteousness, people not being in a place of worthiness and blessing. In the New Covenant in Jesus, the curse has been removed! God only has blessing for His children. He is only going to bless you. Look at Jesus' life. Not once did Jesus ever curse a person, not even the people who hated Him. Of course, many chose to live without His blessing, but His heart toward them was for a blessed life. Jesus blesses you today! To be blessed means that you are going up, not going down. It means that your life is increasing in its goodness, not decreasing. It means that more and more of the life of God is manifesting in you, not less and less. To think of your life as cursed, believer, is to think differently about your life than God thinks. How will you be able to receive God's blessing for you if your thinking and beliefs are diametrically opposed to God's thinking and beliefs? Why not agree with Him about your life? God is a blessing God, and you are the object of His blessing.

. . . .

Prayer of Agreement

Father, I believe what You say, that You are a blessing God and that You are blessing my life today. I raise up my head today to expect Your blessings to manifest. I receive Your way of thinking about me, and I look forward to seeing more and more of Your blessings come into my life.

You Can Understand
How God Thinks Toward You

"For 'who has known the mind of the Lord that he may instruct Him?' But we have the mind of Christ."
—*1 Corinthians 2:16*

It's a startling thought that, as a believer, you have the ability to understand and believe God's thoughts and intentions toward you. The Bible says, *"'Eye has not seen, nor ear heard, nor has it entered into the heart of man the things which God has prepared for those who love Him.' But God has revealed them to us through His Spirit" (1 Corinthians 2:9–10).* You have the ability today to think the way Jesus thinks about you! A lot of believers don't think as Jesus thinks because they're just not used to thinking in such positive ways about themselves and about their Father. We gravitate toward negative thinking, like, *Nothing will ever change for me.* Or, *My life is a sinking ship, I'll never get ahead, I'll never be healed, I'll never feel loved.* Those thoughts and beliefs contradict what Jesus thinks about you. If you want God's goodness to manifest in your life, you need to begin thinking like Jesus. And you can! Here is a liberating thought: You can choose your thoughts on purpose! Your thoughts don't have to be driven by negative thinking ruts in your brain. You have the mind of Christ! Begin thinking like Jesus thinks, "that you're loved, you're worthy, you're valuable, you're blessed."

. . . .

Prayer of Agreement

Jesus, I believe what You say about me, that I have Your mind inside of me. I can think Your thoughts and understand Your intentions toward me. I choose to believe that You are loving and good and that I am precious to You. Thank You, Holy Spirit, for helping me to change my thinking.

The Lord *Keeps You*

"For this reason I also suffer these things; nevertheless I am not ashamed, for I know whom I have believed and am persuaded that He is able to keep what I have committed to Him until that Day."

—2 Timothy 1:12

God is "keeping" you unto eternal life. He has defined himself as the One who *blesses you and keeps you* (see Numbers 6:24). Jesus, in His prayer to the Father, said, *". . .I kept them in Your name. Those whom You gave Me I have kept."* (John 17:12). Jesus kept them. It wasn't the disciples' job to keep themselves. Jesus kept them from being lost by keeping them "in the name" (in the identity) of the Father. God has taken the responsibility upon Himself to make sure that you are never snatched from His hand. We need to see this, or we will not be able to find our rest before Him. The scripture testifies clearly, *"The LORD is your keeper"* (Psalm 121:5). The apostle Paul became convinced of this. He said, *"I know whom I have believed."* He was saying, in effect, "I am convinced in the integrity of God's character to do what He says He will do." Paul, from prison, had no way to visit the churches he had begun all across the Roman Empire. But He knew that those people would be okay, because he knew the Lord promised to keep them, and he was convinced of God's integrity to keep His promise. Do you believe this for yourself, that the Lord is your Keeper? Do you believe that, in spite of the ups and downs of your faith, and the good and bad deeds you commit of, the Lord will never allow you to be snatched from His hand? The truth is, *"The Lord blesses you and keeps you."* He is your Keeper!

. . . .

Prayer of Agreement
I believe You, Father, that You are my Keeper!
I will stop worrying that I have blown it with
You, because You keep me secure every day in
Your hands. Thank You that this causes me to
find my rest in You. Thank You for loving me
and seeing me as so precious to You.

Christ Living *as You*

"I have been crucified with Christ; it is no longer I who live, but Christ lives in me; and the life which I now live in the flesh I live by faith in the Son of God, who loved me and gave Himself for me."

—*Galatians 2:20*

Jesus prayed in the Garden that we would be one with Him and the Father. This is what happened when His Spirit entered you on the day that you believed in Him. Believers are *"one spirit with Him"* (1 Corinthians 6:17). This is where you find your confidence to do the works of Christ. If you think that your life and Christ's life are two separate lives, it will be impossible for the deepest belief to rise up in you and allow you to speak as Jesus with His authority in the world. You will always perceive yourself (in that mix of your life and Jesus' life) to be the weak link in the chain, the weak rung in the ladder. But think about it: If the chain is all Christ, if the ladder is all Christ, then there is no weak link, and no weak rung. The life that is yours is not you and Christ. It's just Christ. It's not the two of you. It's the one of you. And as we believe this, we begin to partake of it. This is the *"nothing shall be impossible to you"* life. This is the *"greater works shall you do than what I have done"* life. This is the *"whatever you ask in My name"* life. Let that sink into your heart, and then live and speak with the authority of Christ today!

. . . .

Prayer of Agreement

Jesus, I believe what You say, that I am one with You. I believe that if I say something, it comes from our oneness. When I declare Your promises, they are spoken out from our oneness. Thank You for this authority in my life!

Rest Your Hope
Fully in His Grace

"Therefore gird up the loins of your mind, be sober, and rest your hope fully upon the grace that is to be brought to you at the revelation of Jesus Christ."

—*1 Peter 1:13*

Here is something for us to do today: **Gird up the loins of our minds**. To "gird up your mind" means to "focus your thinking around this core understanding." **Be sober**. Being sober in this context is not talking about alcohol. Rather, it's a metaphor that means, "Think clearly about." Be sober means, "Get ready to use all your gray matter for this!" And here is what it's all about: "**Rest your hope fully upon the grace that is to be brought to you at the revelation [or revealing] of Jesus Christ.**" Rest all of your hope (hope is tuned in to the future—it's what we are expecting to come later today, tomorrow, and next week). Rest your hope fully upon the grace that is brought to you at the revealing of Jesus Christ. When Jesus is revealed to you, it's good news! The gospel of grace in Jesus causes you to expect God's goodness. Let that gospel go down deep in you. It's a different way to think. It is not like the depressing thinking of this world that says, "I am unworthy. I have not done enough. How can You love me? Why in the world would You bless me?" That may be normal thinking for the unbelieving world that puts no stock in the "It Is Finished" work of Jesus. But for you who rest your hope fully on grace, your thinking is positive for the future. *"Surely goodness and mercy shall follow me all the days of my life."* Expect it!

. . . .

Prayer of Agreement

Jesus, I believe in Your finished work on the cross for me. Today I choose to focus my mind like a laser on the grace that comes to me when You are truly revealed in my life. I have great hope for Your goodness and mercy to show up in my life today, and tomorrow, and always! Thank You for Your amazing grace!